café culture

THE DEFINITIVE GUIDE TO NORTH WEST

TEA ROOMS, CAFES, AND FISH & CHIP RESTAURANTS

THE DEFINITIVE GUIDE TO
NORTH WEST FISH & CHIP RESTAURANTS,
TEA ROOMS, AND CAFES

∞

LEEDS LIVERPOOL CANAL, UPPERMILL

Built to link the cities of Liverpool and Leeds, the Leeds & Liverpool Canal is the longest canal in Britain built as a single waterway. Known for its rural walks, noteworthy heritage and peaceful boating, its 127 mile length has a lot to offer.

Photography credit: David Schofield

FOREWORD

The North West has got to be one of the most interesting and beautiful regions of Great Britain. From the majestic coast and Morecambe Bay to our wonderful and varied countryside, charming villages, towns and dynamic cities.

Positioned across the region our cafés, which are family owned, have great passion for good food and service. Using fantastic locally sourced produce, their home cooking is of the highest standard and served by friendly northern folk at realistic prices.

When visiting these, our favourite North West quality cafés, we have always been given a very warm welcome and met with genuine hospitality. We feel sure you will be received in exactly the same way. We hope you enjoy your visits.

Victoria Greenwood and Emilia Greenwood

CONTENTS

―――

TEA ROOMS, CAFES, AND FISH & CHIP RESTAURANTS

∞
PLOVER SCAR LIGHTHOUSE

*Also known as the Abbey
Lighthouse, Plover Scar
Lighthouse is an active
19th century lighthouse
that is sited at the entrance
of the Lune estuary, near
Cockersand Abbey in
Lancashire. Easily accessible
from the beach if you want
to have a closer look.*

Photography credit: Robert McEwen

"We always call here when in the area, the best fish and chips in the whole of Cumbria and Lancashire, in our opinion... service is spot on and the food is really first class. Would recommend it to everyone."

Arnside Chip Shop and the Big Chip Café

Arnside

Arnside is a beautiful little civil parish village sat on the estuary of the river Kent, the area is a designated area of natural beauty (AONB) and there are many lovely scenic walks with coastal views to take in. The Arnside chip shop overlooks the estuary and on a nice day you can call in to the takeaway and enjoy your fish and chips in the seating area looking out at the beautiful scenery.

It also offers a chance for customers to sit in its recently refurbished restaurant and has an extensive menu offering not only perfectly fried fish and chips (with gluten free batter option available) but also traditional fare such as scampi, traditional fish cake, sausages, burgers, a range of vegetarian options and a latest addition to the menu a 'seafood basket'. For those wanting to try something a little bit different they have battered Scottish haggis or battered white or black pudding. To finish there are hot and cold sweets available and ice-cream.

Opening times:

Tues to Thur 11.30am—1.45pm and 4.30—7.30pm
Fri 11.30—2 and 4.30—8pm
Sat 11.30—8pm
Sun noon—7pm

Address and contact details:

1 The Promenade, Arnside,
Carnforth LA5 0HF
Telephone: 01524 761 874
www.arnsidechipshop.co.uk

Directions:

Take the B5282 from Milnthorpe to Arnside. The café is on the left had side opposite the estuary.

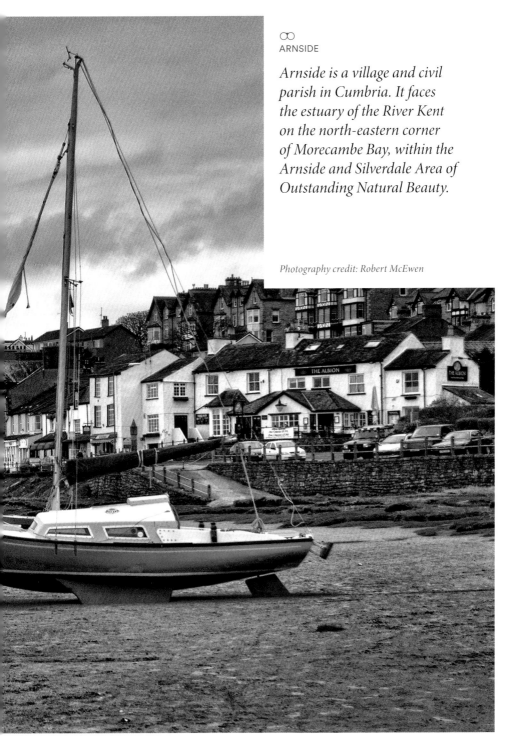

∞

ARNSIDE

Arnside is a village and civil parish in Cumbria. It faces the estuary of the River Kent on the north-eastern corner of Morecambe Bay, within the Arnside and Silverdale Area of Outstanding Natural Beauty.

Photography credit: Robert McEwen

RSPB Leighton Moss Café

Silverdale

The RSPB at Leighton moss has been established for over 50 years, and has the largest reedbed in northwest England. It is therefore home to many marsh dwelling species. Bearded tits and marsh harriers can be seen all year round, making seasonal appearances are bitterns and avocets. There are many trails and walks around the reserve, if you're lucky you may see an otter or a dear along the way.

The café, situated within the converted barn, and has a colourful light and inviting feel. The breakfast menus is served from 9.30am until 11.30am, followed by lunch where a selection of wraps, paninis, sandwiches and baked potato are available, along with daily specials and cakes. All the food is locally sourced, seasonal and free range where possible. There is also the gift shop in the visitors centre.

Opening times:

Café and shop
9.30am—5pm (closing at 4.30pm in December and January)

Address and contact details:

Myers Farm, Storrs Lane,
Silverdale, LA5 0SW
Telephone: 01524 701 601
www.rspb.org.uk

Directions:

Take M6 north, at J35 take A601/A6 to Carnforth, then follow signs for Milnthorpe. Continue on A6 north you will pick up brown tourist signs for the reserve.

"We always make a point of calling in at Leighton Moss on our way down from Scotland, not only for the fantastic wildlife, but to have lunch in this outstanding café."

"Greenlands farm is my favourite place to visit on Sunday lunchtime. Wellies café is great, and the animals are super friendly. The whole place is fab. My 5 year old loves it."

Greenlands Farm Village

Carnforth

At Greenlands Farm Village there is so much for everyone to enjoy, you will be spoilt for choice. If you fancy a day out with the children there is the fantastic Open Farm which is very hands on with plenty of animals to see and pet, they have a large soft play area called The Play Barn, an outdoor undercover play area, and lots to see and do. There are many retail, gift and culinary outlets on-site. Northern Archery for a forest archery experience (booking advisable), Woodcrest Garden Centre, Fawcetts Country Sport Limited, Woodcock & Snipe, Tammi Upton Hair & Nails, Madam Chocolate, Love Cheesecake, Apricot Whirl and Little Curiosity.

When you need to refuel before continuing your day, you will be welcomed in Wellies café, a place to truly relax with your family and friends, they serve full English breakfast (until 11.30am) with vegetarian and lighter options available. For lunch a large selection of homemade main meals along with sandwiches, salads and pizza. For those seeking that little something extra special, there is The Loft Tearoom which is a gorgeous vintage style setting offering homemade food and delicious fresh homemade cakes, deluxe afternoon teas, with a selection of specialty leaf teas, Barista coffees and luxury hot chocolate. For that special occasion, wine, prosecco or champagne is available, (this can also be hired for any celebrations).

Opening times:

Café
Mon to Sun 10am—5pm

Farm
Mon to Sun 10am—4pm

Admissions
Free admission to the café and farm shop
Open farm is £6 per person
Play barn is £5 per person

Address and contact details:

Tewitfield, Carnforth,
Lancashire LA6 1JH
Telephone: 01524 784 184
www.greenlandsfarmvillage.co.uk

Directions:

Close to J35 on the M6. From the motorway take the exit signed for Morecambe, Carnforth and Milnthorpe. After ½ mile you come to a roundabout on the A6, take the second exit for Milnthorpe A6. After a further ½ mile at the roundabout take the second exit signed A6070 for Burton in Kendal. After another ½ mile you cross the motorway and the entrance to Greenlands Village is another 300 yards on your left.

∞
LANCASTER

With its history based on its port and canal, Lancaster is an ancient settlement, dominated by Lancaster Castle, Lancaster Priory Church and the Ashton Memorial Lancaster. It is also the settlement that gives Lancashire its name.

Photography credit: Robert McEwen

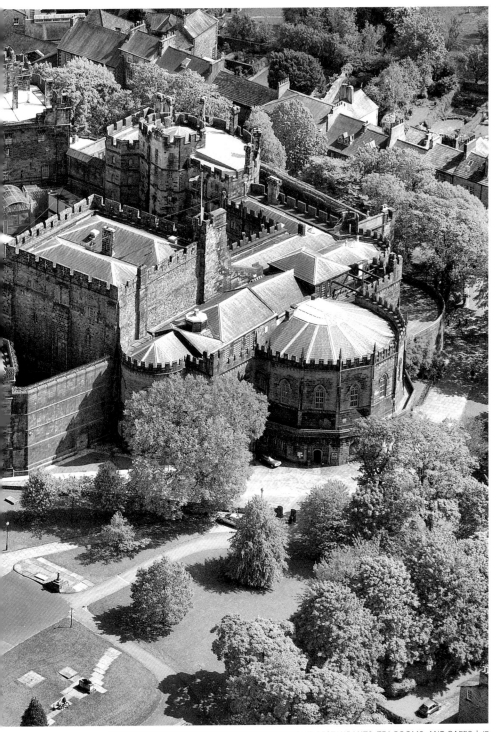

Countrystyle Meats Farm Shop

Lancaster

Open 7 days a week, Countrystyle Meats Farm Shop is a family run business with over 12 years experience in selling quality meats and produce. With growing interest and demand for their quality produce they have recently expanded their business to include an ice cream parlour and large restaurant.

Passionate about supporting local farmers and auction marts, the sizeable butchers counter offers hand selected cuts of meat which are featured on the restaurant's menu. The Farm Shop also offers seasonal fruit & veg, breads and dairy items, jams, chutneys and preserves as well as wines, cheeses, homemade pies and much more. The ice-cream parlour features 24 different flavours of ice cream which is a great treat for both young and old.

With the addition of the restaurant 'Countrystyle Kitchen' customers can now taste the great quality produce sold in the farm shop. The carvery, available 7 days a week, offers cuts of meat roasted to perfection, with a generous range of seasonal veg and all the trimmings (served from 12pm onwards). The carvery runs alongside an extensive à la carte menu which offers an all-day breakfast, fish and chips, and various steaks, along with lighter options including sandwiches, platters, nibbles and homemade soup to name but a few. Countrystyle's afternoon tea has a selection of freshly made finger sandwiches with various fillings, cakes and homemade scones served with jam, clotted cream and Jersey butter. This is accompanied by a selection of fine teas, tisanes or coffee, and for an extra special treat you can add a glass of prosecco or champagne.

Opening times:

Mon to Sat 8.30am—5.30pm
Sun 10.30am—4.30pm

 Address and contact details:

Lancaster Leisure Park,
Wyresdale Road, Lancaster
LA1 3LA
Telephone: 01524 841 111
www.countrystylemeats.co.uk

Directions:

Follow M6 towards Lancaster, exit at J33 and take the A6 exit to south Lancaster. Continue to follow the A6 for about 7 miles, then turn right onto Hazelrigg Lane, continue for 3 miles then turn right onto Langthwaite Road. Continue for 1 mile then turn left onto Pottery Gardens Street (Lancaster Leisure Park). Countrystyle Meats is on the left hand side.

"We had our tea around 3.30pm there. A really good feed from an excellent carvary served up by Alan. He and his staff make sure you have a great meal and good experience."

"Excellent food and service. Highly recommended and produces from Bowland Outdoor Reared farm."

Bridge House Farm

Wray

Bridge House Farm was a working farm until 2004, and sits beside the river Roeburn and Hindburn in the picturesque village of Wray. The fully licensed tearoom is in the converted stone barn, with exposed oak beams and log burning fires for the winter, and ample outdoor seating with a children's play area and a large grass verge on the banks of the river.

The menu is a combination of modern and wholesome traditional Lancashire cuisine, which is kept seasonal, using the best locally sourced produce, and their own meat and eggs. There is a specials board which changes daily, along with a selection of homemade cakes. They serve fresh Illy coffee and stock a good range of wines and beers.

Their sister company Bowland Pork was started in 1995 and has quickly established an excellent reputation. This comes from the quality care, lush grazing in the forest of Bowland and natural diet, providing great tasting meats. They offer beef, pork, lamb and poultry expertly butchered and prepared by the family, all are available to buy in the tearoom, as well as from the farm, and registered stockists.

To make any occasion a memorable one they provide a hog roast service, which they bring to your venue and cater for you.

Opening times:

Summer
Tues to Sun 10am—5pm

Winter
Tues to Sun 10am—4pm

Address and contact details:

Bridge House, Lancaster
LA2 8QP
Telephone: 01524 222 496
www.bowlandpork.co.uk

Directions:

Follow A683 from Heysham towards Wray. Continue for 12½ miles and turn right onto B6480. Continue for just over 1½ miles. Turn right onto Home Farm Close, and Bridge House Farm is ¼ mile up on the left hand side.

Pilling Pottery

Pilling

CLOSED

Pilling pottery serve an all-day breakfast along with homemade pot pies, jacket potatoes and generously filled baguettes. They also have specials which change regularly and homemade soup and cake. Afternoon tea is available throughout the day but booking is essential. However this place is about much more than good food and coffee, it can be thought of as a gym for the mind, a place to come and unwind and let that touch of creativity out.

With a host of activities available such as paint a pot, lessons on the potter's wheel, and hand modelling on the bench (all need pre-booking). They also offer a range of night school courses. On-site there are collections of work from various ceramicists for sale, and commissions are available to order. They stock a range of clays and glazes which you can take home to model with, and bring back to have fired. All work done requires firing and is not available to take home on the same day, however it can be sent to you by post once it is complete.

Their sister company Northern Kilns build and supplies kilns for many different applications.

Opening times:

Open 7 days
Weekdays 11am—3pm
Sat to Sun 10am—4pm

Address and contact details:

School Lane, Pilling,
Garstang, Lancashire
PR3 6HB
Telephone: 01253 799 928
www.pillingpottery.com
cafe@pillingpottery.com
shop@pillingpottery.com
info@northernkilns.com

Directions:

Follow the M6 towards Lancaster. Exit at J33, take A6 exit to Lancaster and pick up A588. Continue for 3½ miles, turn right onto Back Sands Lane, continue onto School Lane. Pilling Pottery is about ½ mile up the lane on the right hand side.

"Went last week for the first time and we loved it. Great food and coffee and lovely people who were very welcoming to us and our dog. Highly recommended."

∞
ST. ANNES PIER, ST ANNES

Lytham St. Annes is internationally renowned for 'British Open' golf tournament. It is a traditional quiet Victorian/Edwardian seaside resort with a sandy beach, donkeys, and small pier. St. Annes Beach also hosts a number of kite flying events each year.

Photography credit: Robert McEwen

The Fish House

Fleetwood

The Fish House is near the dock and freeport in Fleetwood, and therefore ideally situated for high quality fresh fish. This establishment has been both area and regional winner at the national fish and chip awards, and the quality of the fish speaks for itself. With mouth-watering flakes encased in light golden batter, served with fluffy chunky chips and tartar sauce, it is an ideal place for a fish supper (gluten free options available).

The restaurant offers everything the takeaway has and more with burgers, baked potatoes and a variety of fish specials, along with hot and cold beverages and traditional steamed puddings. They will even deliver orders to local caravan parks and holiday sites.

They have a second shop which is a takeaway in Poulton called The Fish Hut.

Opening times:

Wed to Sat 11.30am—9pm
Sun 12—7pm
Mon to Tues 11.30am—9pm

 Address and contact details:

The Fish House,
172-180 Dock Street, Fleetwood
FY7 6NY
Telephone: 01253 779 229

The Fish Hut,
294A Poulton Road, Fleetwood
FY7 6TF

Directions:

Exit M6 at junction 32, pick up M55 continue for 7 miles. At junction 3, take the A585 exit to Kirkham/Fleetwood continue for 11 miles to Dock Street, Fleetwood.

St. Annes Fish Restaurant

Lytham St. Annes

St. Annes Fish Restaurant, has been in the family since 1928 and as such has a long standing great reputation. The current owner is the 4th generation of fish fryers who worked as a chef at many well-known establishments before taking over the business. All the pies pudding and desserts are homemade using only the best local ingredients, with many GF options available.

The licensed dining room has a traditional feel, which is steeped in history through photos on the wall. There is outside seating available and good disabled access to both the restaurant and the takeaway. The restaurant is 800 yards from the sea front where you can relax on the beach, visit the arcade, and stroll round the local shops. It lies just two miles away from the sea side holiday towns of Lytham and Blackpool, if you fancy an extended visit.

Opening times:

Mon to Thurs 11.30am—1.30pm then 4.30—8pm
Fri to Sat 11.45am—8pm
Sun Closed

Address and contact details:

41 St Andrew's Road South,
Lytham St. Annes FY8 1PZ
Telephone: 01253 723 311
www.stannesfishrestaurant.co.uk

Directions:

Follow the B5233 towards Lytham St. Annes for approximately 1 mile, then turn left onto St. Andrews Road South. St. Annes Fish Restaurant is along this road on the left.

The Courtyard Caffé

Great Eccleston

The Courtyard Caffé is set in the beautiful civil parish village of Great Eccleston, just south of the river Wyre near the Fylde coast. The café is light and airy with white marble tables and comfy seating. A secluded courtyard at the back where you can relax in the warm summer months, and seating to the front so you can watch the world go by.

Full English breakfast is available along with lighter options, poached egg or crumpets. There is a selection of hot and cold sandwiches, soups and paninis, along with main meals such as Whitby scampi and chips. Afternoon tea is also served which has a choice of sandwiches, homemade scones with preserve and cream along with tea, coffee, or fizz if you prefer. There is also a selection of homemade cakes.

 Opening times:

Tues to Sat 9am—4.30pm
Sun 10am—4pm

 Address and contact details:

17 High Street, Great Eccleston,
Preston, PR3 0ZB
Telephone: 01995 672 011
www.thecourtyardcaffebar.co.uk

Directions:

Follow Garstang Road A586 from Blackpool towards Preston. Turn right on to the B5293, the Courtyard Caffé is along this road on the right.

∞
BLACKPOOL PROMENADE

The famous Lancashire seaside resort of Blackpool is still a favourite with day trippers and holidaymakers. With its trams, illuminations, the golden mile, three piers, the Pleasure Beach and Blackpool Tower, you will never run out of fun things to do.

Photography credit: Robert McEwen

Light Ash Farm

Bilsborrow

Light ash farm a is family run business set in their converted barn, offering wood burning fires to cosy up to in winter and outside seating for those lovely summer days. Situated in beautiful country side near the river Brock, there are scenic views, with plenty of wildlife, and walks around the farm and surrounding public foot paths.

The breakfast menu (served until 11.30am) which runs alongside the main menu offers a hearty full English, with lighter options available. The main menu has a selection of hot and cold sandwiches, salads, and main meals, along with a varied specials board including homemade soups which regularly changes, and are all made with fresh local produce.

For dessert there is an extensive cake range to choose from all homemade on-site, and if you're feeling a little full they are available to take away. Celebration cakes can be made to order for that special occasion, and outside catering provided as well.

Afternoon tea is served from 2pm on a traditional tiered stand with a selection of finger sandwiches, dainty homemade cakes and delicious fresh scones. The farm shop sells fresh local produce, giftware, and haberdashery.

Opening times:

Thurs to Mon 10—4pm

Address and contact details:

St Michael's Road, Bilsborrow, Preston PR3 0RT
Telephone: 01995 640 068
www.lightashfarmshop.co.uk

Directions:

Follow the A6 from Broughton towards Bilsborrow for 3½ miles. Turn left on to St. Michaels Road. Continue for 1½ miles Light Ash Farm will be signposted on the right hand sign.

In May 2015, Light Ash Farm had the huge honour of serving lunch to Her Royal Highness Queen Elizabeth.

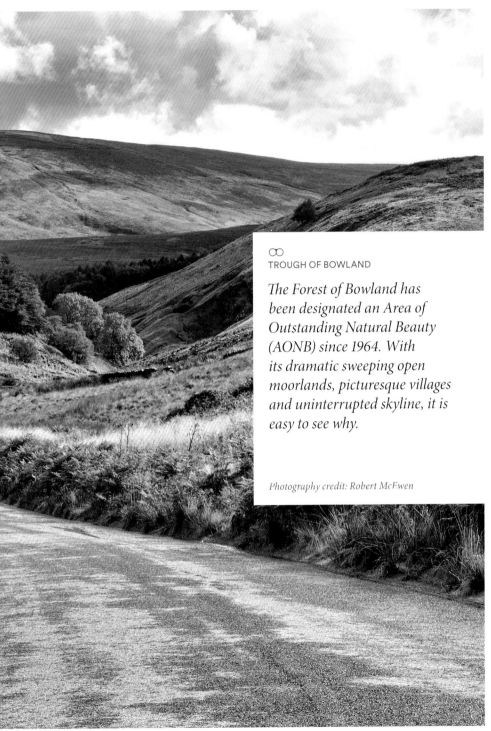

∞
TROUGH OF BOWLAND

The Forest of Bowland has been designated an Area of Outstanding Natural Beauty (AONB) since 1964. With its dramatic sweeping open moorlands, picturesque villages and uninterrupted skyline, it is easy to see why.

Photography credit: Robert McEwen

Garstang Fish and Chip Shop

Garstang

Garstang Fish and Chips is found in the centre of the quaint market town of Garstang. Having opened in August 2013 it has built up a great reputation very quickly with its quality products and location. It is a traditional fish and chip shop, serving only the best sustainably caught fish available, and uses locally grown potatoes. All the fish are filleted and chips produced on-site daily.

As well as a modern takeaway there is also a 50 seater restaurant with a more traditional feel, with exposed beams and clean decoration. The owner was named best male Young Fish Fryer of the Year in 2014 and his food certainly lives up to the award. The shop was also named in the Best 50 Fish and Chips shops in 2016.

The shop is situated next to a large free car park, and is wheel-chair accessible. There are plenty of nice walks around Garstang and the high street has many independently run shops that are worth a visit.

Opening times:

Mon to Sat 11.30—2pm
and 4.30—8pm
Sun 4—9.30pm

Address and contact details:

Stoops Hall Wind, Garstang,
Preston PR3 1EA
Telephone: 01995 600 205

Directions:

Follow A6 from Preston to Garstang for 14 miles, then turn right onto Moss Lane. At the roundabout take 1st exit onto B6430. Garstang Fish and Chips will be along here on the right.

"Staff were friendly, food was excellent and a very clean place to eat would definitely come back here to eat when in Garstang again."

Cobble Hey Farm and Gardens

Claughton-on-Brock

Cobble hay farm and garden has something for everyone, in the spring there are several breeds of lamb to feed and pet, along with calves, goats and pigs. They are part of the nature conservation act and work closely with the RSPCA to protect local native breeds of bird, especially wetland birds such as lapwing, curlews snipe etc; they also have a lapwing walk and bird watching area.

The farm has many facilities including a large indoor play barn, and outdoor play areas. Beautiful gardens with a variety of hardy plants grown on the farm, along with a sensory garden. They have a café serving good home cooked food using meat and vegetables from the farm or very locally sourced. In the colder months you can warm by the log fire, and there is an outdoor seating area for warm summer days.

Cobble hey believes in access for all visitors with electric wheelchairs available, and a tramper available to book. They also have a separate room which can be booked for parties, conferences and meetings etc.

Opening times:

Thurs to Sun 10.30—4.30pm
Open on Bank Holidays

Address and contact details:

Forest of Bowland AONB,
Hobbs Lane, Claughton-on-Brock,
Garstang, Preston PR3 0QN
Telephone: 01995 602 643
www.cobblehey.co.uk
There is a small entry fee for access to the farm.

Directions:

From Lancaster take the M6 to J33, then follow the A6 towards Garstang until you see the garage on your left, then follow the brown tourist signs, which will either be named Cobble Hey Gardens or the flower symbol. Cobble Hey Farm and Gardens is approximately 3 miles from the junction.

"One of the best days out we've had! Friendly owner, beautiful setting, amazing gardens and the animals made the day perfect! The lunch we had in the tea room was fresh and delicious, and we will be going back soon. Next time, I'm going to walk one of the goats!"

The Potting Shed

Longridge

With a rustic, homely yet quirky feel The Potting Shed is somewhere you can relax and enjoy delightful food. In the summer months you can sit in the roof garden and take in the surrounding countryside.

A full English breakfast is served until 11.30am along with smoked salmon and scrambled egg, or granola. For lunch a delightful selection of homemade burgers which are a refreshingly healthy change from the norm, with vegetarian and vegan options available. Beautifully indulgent salads both warm and cold bursting with greens, beans and fruits. Wholesome main meals are also served along with the specials board which changes regularly, and a tempting selection of locally made cakes.

The afternoon tea is a beautiful assortment of dainty delights including sandwiches, homemade scones, and cakes all set out on a traditional tired cake stand, this comes with tea or coffee. And for the more savoury pallet, a picnic basket filled with cheeses, home cooked hams, frittata and much more can be had. Downstairs there is a garden centre, selling shrubs, bedding plants, pots, garden wear and tools. It also has a pretty little shop with ornaments and occasional gifts.

Opening times:

Tue to Sat 10am—5pm

Address and contact details:

Spout Farm Nursery,
140 Preston Road, Longridge,
Preston PR3 3BD
Telephone: 01772 780 590
www.thepottingshedlongridge.co.uk

Directions:

Situated approximately 3 miles along the B6243 from Preston to Longridge on the right hand side.

"Visited yesterday for lunch had the ploughman's and chips to share with a friend. It was excellent wasn't sure how big it was going to be so we thought we could have a piece of cake after, but didn't need to worry portion was big enough for both it was delicious. Will definitely be going back with other friends and family."

∞
PENDLE HILL

Dominating the Forest of Bowland AONB, and standing between the districts of Pendle and Ribble Valley, Pendle Hill's history dates back as far as the Bronze Age as an ancient burial ground was found at the summit.

Photography credit: John Toms

The Café at Stydd Gardens

Ribchester

Stydd Gardens is situated in the ancient Roman town of Ribchester in the beautiful Ribble Valley. This enchanting place has a unique feel that you just can't quite put your finger on. The café bar/tearoom is housed in an enchanting Mediterranean style green house, laid out with climbing grape vines, and shabby chic furnishings it's a truly relaxing atmosphere. All the food at Stydd is made with fresh local produce, combined to bringing invigorating flavours, along with traditional favourites. Breakfast (served 10 until 11am), lunch (served from noon–4.30pm) and the sumptuous Best of British afternoon tea (available between 3.00–4.30pm booking essential.

The gardens at Stydd are beautifully landscaped, inspirational and thought provoking to walk around. Within these grounds there are several small independent businesses, each with its own unique creative style. Boho Kisses Boutique, Pasharah Designs, Lavendula, Maison De Lamond, The Wine Shed, The Bee Garden and Rosie Duck.

Opening times:

Tues to Sun 10.00am—4.30pm

Address and contact details:

Stoneygate Lane, Ribchester, Preston PR3 3YN
Telephone: 01254 820 120
www.stydd.com

Directions:

Follow the B6245 from Blackburn towards Ribchester for about 4 miles, turn right onto Ribblesdale Road and continue for about ¼ mile then Stydd Gardens will be on the right hand side.

"Set in the beautiful Ribble valley in the Roman village of Ribchester. 1st class views with a 1st class service. Can't wait to go back. Thank you everybody for making my visit perfect."

∞
BROCK BOTTOM

Brock Bottom, also known as Brock Picnic Area, Brock Valley, Brock Mill and Brock Valley Nature Trail, are all different names usually referring to the area along the River Brock, from the picnic spot which is just off Brock Mill Lane, in the Forest of Bowland AONB.

Photography credit: Paul Grogan Photography

The Bobbin Café

Burnley

The licensed Bobbin café is set in the heart of the weavers' triangle in Burnley, and this theme is echoed throughout the décor with bobbins, looms and spinning wheels hanging on the walls. You can start your day with a satisfying weavers' breakfast, or a lighter bite if you prefer (served until 11.45am). For lunch a tempting selection of sandwiches, paninis and main meals are, along with a good selection of daily specials, and why not finish with one of their home made desserts. Afternoon tea is served from 2pm–4pm which includes a selection of homemade mini sweets savouries all served on a wooden board.

The mill shop sells beautiful fabrics, for all your furnishing needs including curtain poles, tiebacks and all the fixture and fitting you need. They also offer a local measuring service and made to measure curtains.

Opening times:

Mon to Sat 9.15am—5pm

Address and contact details:

Oakmount Mill,
Wiseman Street, Burnley
BB11 1RU
Telephone: 01282 436 462
www.finefabrics-burnley.co.uk

Directions:

Take the M65 to Burnley and exit at J10. Take A671 and continue for about ½ mile, turn right on to Wiseman Street, the Bobbin Café is up this street on the right.

Greendale View

Chatburn

With breath taking views overlooking the Ribble Valley this is place to relax and unwind. During the winter you can sit by the wood burning fire, and in the summer months this stunning scenery can be enjoyed in the garden.

Arriving early in the morning the smell of organic homemade bread fills the air, and this can be enjoyed with anything from a full English including Farnworth sausage and free range eggs, to simple jam on toast. For lunch hot and cold sandwiches with various filling, along with baked potatoes and platters are available. There is a specials board offering hearty main meals and seasonal homemade soups, all ingredients are locally sourced and organic where possible.

Afternoon tea is served as a platter with rustic sandwiches on organic homemade bread, along with scones, and cakes which are all baked fresh daily. This comes with a salad garnish, homemade coleslaw and tea, coffee or a glass of prosecco.

Opening times:

Mon to Sat 8am—5pm
Sun available to book for functions

Address and contact details:

Forest of Bowland AONB,
Downham Road, Chatburn,
Clitheroe BB7 4DL
Telephone: 01200 441 517

Directions:

From Clitheroe take the road to Chatburn, in the village turn right onto Downham Road over the dual carriageway. Greendale View is on the left hand side.

Holden Clough Nursery and The Garden Kitchen

Bolton-by-Bowland

Holden Clough Nursery has a warm, friendly and inviting feel, with spacious rooms to dine in and sofas to relax and have a chat on. A hearty gardener's breakfast with lighter options is available from 10.00–11.15am. They serve a good selection of sandwiches, salads, platters and paninis along with hot meals too. A good gluten free menu is offered, alongside specials that change daily, and warming homemade soup which is always changing too. Finish off with a tempting selection of homemade desserts, and a range of hot and cold beverages including wines and beers.

The afternoon picnic is a must try. With a variety of miniature savouries and sweets, made in quaint little pots and mini welly boots, all served on a 'miniature picnic table'!

The shop in the entrance has an interesting little selection of sweet treats and dried goods, as well as cooking oils and ornaments. The nursery has a beautiful range of shrubs, bedding plants, and hanging baskets for those of you looking to add a splash of colour to your garden.

Opening times:

Mon to Fri 10.00am—4.30pm
Sat and Sun 9.30—5.30

Address and contact details:

Holden, Bolton-by-Bowland,
Lancashire BB7 4PF
Telephone: 01200 447 447
www.holdencloughnursery.com

Directions:

Take the A59 to Sawley, take the Sawley turning onto Sawley Road, turn left at the Spread Eagle, follow this road around to the right continue along this lane (you will pick up signs for Holden Clough). Turn left onto Holden Lane. Holden Clough Nursery and The Garden Kitchen is along this lane on the left.

"Lovely picnic enjoyed by my parents. I had an enjoyable lunch too in a beautiful setting. It was a gorgeous sunny afternoon with some beautiful flowers and plants on display."

∞
SLAIDBURN

Slaidburn is a village and civil parish within the Ribble Valley district of Lancashire, England. With a population in 2001 of just under 300, increasing to 351 at the 2011 Census, the parish covers just over 5,000 acres of the Forest of Bowland.

Photography credit: Victoria Greenwood

Riverbank Tearooms

Slaidburn

The Riverbank Tearoom sits on the banks of the river Hodder in the Forest of Bowland. It is a beautiful spot to relax and enjoy the scenery of the river and peaceful surrounding countryside, or have a walk around the picturesque village of Slaidburn. The tearoom has a cosy upstairs seating area where a selection of hot and cold sandwiches is available along with wholesome main meals such as deep filled cheese and onion pie, all day breakfast, and braised pork loin.

There are delicious specials, which vary daily made using the best quality locally sourced produce from Bowland meats and other local businesses. They also have a selection of freshly baked scones, tempting sponge cakes and fruit pies, which can be enjoyed after a meal, or with a beverage of your choice including a glass of wine or bottled beer. This is a truly beautiful area with outside seating available for those nice days.

Opening times:

Tue to Sun 9.30am—5pm
(just cakes and drinks after
4.30pm)

Address and contact details:

23 Chapel Street, Slaidburn,
Clitheroe, Lancashire BB7 3ES
Telephone: 01200 446 398
www.riverbanktearooms.co.uk

Directions:

Situated on the B6478 from
Clitheroe to Long Preston,
near Slaidburn village on the
left hand side.

∞

SCALEBAR FORCE, SETTLE

Situated just off High Hill Lane, a minor road between Settle and Malham in the Yorkshire Dales, the waterfall is hardly visible from the road. Accessed from a roadside stile, then down a path and some rather steep steps, it is one of the photographer's favourite waterfalls in Yorkshire.

Photography credit: Paul Grogan Photography

Be A Garden Maker Nectar Tearoom

Wigglesworth (near Settle)

Nectar tearoom has a warm and inviting feel with wood burning stove glowing and various pieces of interest to look at. Or you can enjoy the views of the garden on a nice day while dining or enjoying a refreshing cider. They have a light breakfast menu along with sandwiches, and main meals of which there are plenty of vegetarian options, there are daily specials such as gammon and chilli along with tempting cakes which are all homemade.

The shop sells various pieces of homeware and gifts. The garden centre is well stocked with seasonal plants many of which are grown on-site. And if you fancy something a little different for the garden, there is a selection of pieces from the reclamation centre which is on-site providing some beautiful ornaments, such as wash tubs, mill stones and large urns along with various metal work pieces.

Opening times:

Tearoom and garden centre
9am—4.30pm

Address and contact details:

Wigglesworth, Skipton
BD23 4SN
Telephone: 01729 840 848
www.beagardenmaker.co.uk

Directions:

Take the A65 from Skipton to Settle. At Long Preston turn left onto the B6478 to Slaidburn. It is through Wigglesworth on the left hand side.

"Food and service excellent, lovely homely room with log burner blazing. We visited on a Sunday afternoon, on a grey day but still managed to have a look around the centre. Well worthy of a visit, food all freshly cooked."

∞
WATLOWES DRY VALLEY, MALHAM

Town End Farm overlooks Malham Cove from the tea room, a visit to Malham and the surrounding areas is a must. With Malham Cove, Gordale Scar, Janet's Foss and Malham Tarn all within a few minutes of each other by car, you can enjoy some of the most dramatic scenery in the UK.

Photography credit: Paul Grogan Photography

Town End Farm

Airton, Skipton

Town End Farm is set in the beautiful surroundings of Malhamdale, where from the tearoom you look out over Malham Cove. It is a warm and spacious setting, with outside seating available for nice days. The café offers a light breakfast served 'til noon, along with main meals using ingredients from the farm itself or very locally sourced, such as Yorkshire Chorizo Quesadilla. They also have a variety of daily specials, and tempting sweets, along with a selection of teas, coffees, wine and Yorkshire ales.

The farm shop stocks various meat reared on the farm, or from neighbouring farms, that are local native breeds. They also have a fantastic range of Charcuterie and Salami all made on-site. A tempting selection of local cheeses, preserves, gins and ales are stocked, and a gift section upstairs for that little something extra special.

There are a range of teaching courses available in Butchery, as well as Salami and Charcuterie making.

Opening times:

Tues to Sat 9.30am—5pm
Sun 10am—5pm
Closed Monday except Bank Holidays
Last orders in the Tearoom 4pm

Address and contact details:

Airton, Skipton, North Yorkshire, BD23 4BE
Telephone: 01729 830 902
info@townendfarmshop.co.uk
www.townendfarmshop.co.uk

Directions:

Take A65 from Skipton to Settle. Follow the signs for, Malham turning right. Then follow signs for Airton, the farm shop is just through Airton on the left hand side.

"Called in for a bite to eat, great food, great service and friendly staff. The shop was well stocked with local produce, well worth the visit would recommend to anyone."

"Been in twice this week already, can't praise the café enough. Great coffee and a delicious flat white... food was great too. Just a walk away from home... think it could become my second office."

Goat Gap Café

Newby

The newly renovated Goat Gap Café has a relaxed, open plan, and stylish feel, and the fresh food theme is at the heart of this establishment with fresh herbs on every table. The menu is an eclectic mix of fresh flavours and simple classics, they have fantastic deli salads served with homemade flatbreads or sourdough, flavoursome main meals full of quality, fresh local produce, and tempting homemade cakes. These can be enjoyed while taking in the views of the Forest of Bowland through the large arch windows.

The Goat Gap Café is at the foot of Ingleborough which features in the three peaks challenge along with Whernside and Pen-Y-Ghent. Its location in front of this majestic giant makes it the ideal starting point or end point for many walks, and has inspired local artist Phillip Corps, whose art work hangs in the café. Being situated directly on the A65 also makes it a popular rest stop for cyclists, and motorists alike, traveling between the Lake District and the Yorkshire Dales.

Opening times:

Mon to Fri 8am—5pm
Sat to Sun 9am—5pm

Address and contact details:

Henbusk Lane, Newby,
Carnforth LA2 8HS
hello@goatgapcafe.co.uk
www.goatgapcafe.co.uk

Directions:

Situated on the A65 between Clapham and Ingleton, the Goat Gap Café is about 1 mile from Clapham.

∞
INGLEBOROUGH MOUNTAIN

The Ingleton Mountain trail is located 8 minutes up the A65 from the Goat Gap Café and offers a well-known circular walk beginning and ending in the village of Ingleton.

Photography credit: Paul Grogan Photography

Embleys Nurseries
The Archers Restaurant and Coffee Shop

Much Hoole

The Arches Restaurant and Coffee Shop at Embleys is a fully licensed restaurant with fresh and inviting style. They serve a hearty full English breakfast, along with lighter options including eggs benedict, and homemade scones (available until 11.30am). For lunch a good selection of sandwiches and lighter bites is available all served with homemade crisps. A mouth-watering selection of wholesome main meals, along with daily specials and homemade soup which change regularly. To finish there is a delicious choice of puddings, cakes and tarts.

The afternoon tea is a wonderful platter of fresh sandwiches, dainty savouries, and tempting homemade cakes, served with tea or coffee. In the nursery they have an extensive range of shrubs, bedding plants, fruit trees and roses, along with many of the tools, furniture and gardening equipment you need, to create your ideal outdoor space.

Opening times:

Nursery
Mon to Sat 9am—5pm
Sun 10am—4pm

Archers
Mon to Sat 9am—4.30pm
Sun 10am—3pm

Address and contact details:

Liverpool Road, Much Hoole,
Preston, Lancashire, PR4 4RL

Telephone numbers:
Nurseries 01772 612 227
The Arches 01772 396 081
www.embleysnurseries.co.uk

Directions:

Embleys Nurseries is around 2 miles out of Longton on the A59 between Preston and Southport.

"Just popped in on my way home and had just a sandwich and tea. It was one of the best cheese and chutney sandwiches that I've had for years and at a reasonable cost. Definitely worth the visit."

"Have been here a few times with my husband, called again with our daughter and she loved it. Enjoyed looking round and finished in the lovely café. Would definitely recommend to all my family and friends."

The Old Corn Mill and Village Pantry

Bretherton

Surrounded by beautiful countryside between Leyland and Southport, this family run antiques centre is a treasure trove for visitors. It has featured on several BBC programs including The BBC Antiques Road Trip

They sell furniture pieces of many types in mahogany, oak, pine and more, including wardrobes, chairs, desks and bookcases. They have an extensive range of clocks, porcelain, jewellery, Art Deco, Art Nouveau, and shabby chić. Within the centre they undertake restoration and renovation including re-upholstering, stripping and French polishing.

Once you have finished browsing, you can enjoy quality home cooked food in the Villages Pantry Tearoom. They serve a full English (until 12 noon) with vegetarian and lighter options available. A good selection of burgers, sandwiches and traditional main meals including GF quiche. The specials board is always changing and offers three homemade soups to choose from. A delightful selection of classic desserts is available to round of you meal, or can simple be enjoyed with a hot or cold beverage of your choice, including Fitzpatrick's, and Fentimans botanical drinks.

They also offer outside catering for any occasion.

 Opening times:

Shop
Mon to Sat 10am—5pm
Sun 11am—5pm

Tearoom
Mon to Sat 10am—4pm
Sun 11am—4pm

Address and contact details:

The Old Corn Mill, 64 South Road, Bretherton, Leyland, PR26 9AH
Telephone: 01772 601 371
www.oldcornmill.co.uk

Directions:

Follow the A59 from Preston heading towards Southport for about 8 miles. Take the B5247 onto Carr House Lane and continue for just over 1 mile. The Old Corn Mill will be on the left hand side at the road junction.

Heskin Farmers Market and Craft Centre

Chorley

Set in the heart of rural Lancashire, Heskin Farmers Market combines over 40 unique shops and businesses to bring you a wonderful shopping experience. You'll find various ladies and gents clothing outlets, jewellers, craft shops, quality butchers, and a leading art gallery, along with bathroom show rooms, wood burning stoves and much more. They are all independent small businesses that bring you the finest gifts and produce.

When you need a break from perusing the many shops, there is the Two Birds Tearoom, which is licensed and serves quality home cooked food. All the meals are made to order, and there is a good selection of salads, paninis and snacks to choose from along with the soup which is made fresh daily. There is a wonderful variety of homemade cakes, good coffee and a selection of teas.

Opening times:

Tues to Sun 10am—5pm

Address and contact details:

Wood Lane, Heskin,
Chorley PR7 5PA
Telephone: 07599 831 907
www.heskinfarmersmarket.co.uk

Directions:

From M6 take junction 27, exit on A5209, take B5250 continue for 3½ miles. Heskin Farmers Market will be on left.

"This is a delightful lunch or snack café, great selection with lots of homemade cakes as well as savouries."

∞
SOUTHPORT

Set in Southport within the beautiful Victoria Park, the British Musical Fireworks Championship is a firework displays like no other. The competition began in 1999, and the entire show is choreographed to music making it a truly spectacular event.

Photography credit: Robert McEwen

"*Beautiful location. Tea room immaculately clean. Staff very friendly. Plenty of variety on the main menu and daily specials in addition. Food absolutely delicious. Will definitely be returning.*"

Scarisbrick Marina and Tearoom

Scarisbrick

The family run marina and tearoom, is set in beautiful countryside between Southport and Ormskirk. As such there is direct access to the Leeds Liverpool canal paths, and lovely walks within the area. The tearoom is situated in front of the jetties of the marina, with both indoor and outside seating available to admire the boats from. Inside the tearoom is a curiosity corner selling small antiques and supplies.

The serve a hearty boaters' breakfast with lighter options available (until 11.30am). Lunch is a selection of traditional wholesome, homemade Lancashire favourites, along with sandwiches, burgers and salads. There is a specials board which regularly changes, including homemade soup of the day, and to satisfy your sweet tooth, there is a good selection of cakes and puddings, which can be enjoyed with tea, coffee or a soft drink including a range of Fentimans beverages.

Opening times:

Mon to Sun 9am—4pm
(cake and drinks only after 3pm)
Closed Monday except
Bank Holidays
Last orders in the Tearoom 4pm

Address and contact details:

Southport Road, Scarisbrick,
Ormskirk L40 8HQ
Telephone: 01704 841 924
www.scarisbrickmarina.com

Directions:

From M6 take J26 towards M58 Skelmersdale/Southport, follow for 5 miles. Exit J3 take A570 exit, follow A570 for 7 miles. The marina will be on the left hand side.

The new marina is located to the west of Scarisbrick Bridge 27A on the A570 Southport Road in Scarisbrick.

∞

SCARISBRICK MARINA

The Leeds and Liverpool Canal is a canal in Northern England, linking the cities of Leeds and Liverpool. The first section of the canal opened from Bingley to Skipton in 1773, and the final section in Bridgewater was completed around 1816. The main cargo at this time would have been coal.

Photography credit: Victoria Greenwood

The Farm Burscough

Burscough

The Farm Burscough is set in rural countryside that lies between Southport and Ormskirk, with Liverpool just a short drive away, making it the ideal place to take a short break. In the century renovated barn 4 star B&B accommodation is available in 3 twin/double rooms with ensuite bathrooms. They have a large camping and caravan site and a camping pod new for 2017, along with shower and toilet facilities.

With The Farm lying in the countryside and backing onto the Leeds Liverpool canal there are plenty of walks to enjoy around the farm and surroundings. Whether staying as a guest or just enjoying one of the many walks, you will find plenty of freshly prepared wholesome food in The Farm's licensed tearoom. A hearty all day breakfast can be had made with their own free range eggs, local bacon and sausage. There are vegetarian and lighter options available. A good selection of traditional lunches are served using vegetables grown on the farm or locally sourced produce. In the farm shop they stock essentials for campers, homemade cakes, pies and chutneys, alongside local, meats, dairy, beers and crisps. There is also Ruby Raggins gift and craft shop, a salon Beauty by Tanya Louise, and J9'K9 dog grooming service.

Opening times:

Mon to Sat 9am—4pm
Sun 10am—4pm
(last hot food orders 3.30pm)

Address and contact details:

71 Martin Lane, Burscough,
Lancashire L40 0RT
Telephone: 01704 894 889
www.thefarmburscough.co.uk

Directions:

From the M6 exit at J27 and pick up A5209 Wigan/Parbold. Continue for 3 miles then turn right on to A59. Continue for ½ mile and turn left onto Higgins Lane, then continue for about 1 mile. Turn left onto Gorst Lane and continue for another mile you will see sign for The Farm Burscough.

"I have had the pleasure of visiting on many occasions and I have to say that I am never disappointed. On our most recent visit we had an afternoon tea which was a delight. A fabulous selection of sandwiches and cakes. The staff are so friendly, helpful and welcoming."

Inglenook Farm Café

Rainford (near St. Helens)

The farmhouse café has three cosy dining areas. They offer an all-day farmhouse breakfast, along with a variety of wholesome main meals and daily specials such as minted lamb and vegetable pie. There are also lighter bites, and a selection of delicious homemade cakes. For that extra special treat a vintage afternoon tea is served from 1.00–3.30pm daily, including sandwiches, fresh scones with jam and clotted cream, and either tea or coffee.

Inglenook farm produce organic lavender and chamomile which they harvest and distil on-site. They also import and process raw plant-based products such as frankincense. These are used to produce premium organic essential oils. There are over 80 oils available in the Essentia Oil shop, including hydrosols and carrier oils. They also offer visits to learn how the oils are produced, and you can even help out during harvest season.

Opening times:

Café
9am—5pm in summer
9am—4pm in winter
(Food served until at 4pm)

Essentia Oils shop
10am—4pm in summer
10am—3pm in winter

 Address and contact details:

Moss Nook Lane, Rainford Bypass
WA11 8AE
Telephone: 01744 886 812
www.inglenook-farm.co.uk
www.essenciaoils.com

Directions:

Follow M6, M58 take J3 to Rainford Road/A570 follow A570 for 3 miles, Inglenook Farm will be on the left hand side.

"It is fabulous. Nothing better than having a lush breakfast outdoors with lavender sprigs on the tables. Then off to make a fuss of Whitey and Lucky before reluctantly leaving. Are we allowed to bring a couple of carrots for Whitey, his eyes always seem to plead for a yummy treat."

Boasting magnificent architecture and the largest group of Grade 1 listed buildings in the UK, including the Albert Dock and the three Graces, Liverpool waterfront mixes rich heritage with modern attractions.

Photography credit: Paul Grogan Photography

Poppins Tearooms

Horwich (near Bolton)

Poppins has an Edwardian inspired style, with beautiful décor, lace table cloths, and chandeliers. A Mary Poppins style bicycle is parked outside and her hat and umbrella are hung on the coat stand. It is the perfect setting for an authentic afternoon tea.

The morning fayre is light but wholesome with eggs benedict, pancakes and fruit porridge to be had. There is a generous selection of original sandwiches, homemade soup and baked potato. There are seven afternoon teas to choose from including Jane and Michael's for the children. This can all be enjoyed with a selection of loose leaf teas, coffees or soft drinks. And for dessert there is a choice of cakes, and puddings.

Opening times:

Mon to Sat 10.00am—5.00pm

Address and contact details:

142 Lee Lane, Horwich,
Bolton BL6 7AF
Telephone: 01204 773 520

Directions:

Situated on the B6226 from Horwich to Bolton, Poppins Tearoom is about 100 yards from A673 on the left hand side.

Fresh Café

Rawtenstall

Fresh is a modern and stylish café sat on the cobbled streets of Rawtenstall town centre. They offer a varied breakfast menu including full English, eggs benedict and muesli served until 11.30am and all day on Sunday. For lunch they have a range of tantalising light snacks, freshly baked breads and pastries, along with fresh deli sandwiches, salads, Italian inspired meals and daily specials

These can all be enjoyed with a hot or cold beverage of your choice including beers, wines and spirits. The dessert menu is an absolute delight with lots of freshly made cakes, tarts and pudding to choose from along with a generous selection of ice-creams. The afternoon tea is a real treat with dainty desserts and savouries arranged on a traditional tiered stand available with tea, coffee or a glass of Prosecco.

Opening times:

Mon to Sat 8.30am—5.30pm
Tue 8.30am—3pm
Sun 9.30am—5pm

Address and contact details:

89 Bank Street, Rawtenstall,
Lancashire BB4 7QN
Telephone: 01706 218 302
www.fresh-deli-rawtenstall.co.uk

Directions:

Follow the A682 from Burnley to Rossendale. Turn left onto Newchurch Road, then immediately right on to Bank Street. Fresh is along here on the left hand side.

Park Farm Shop and Tearoom

Walmersley (near Ramsbottom)

This family run, licensed tearoom, has traditional 120-seater dining area. It serves wholesome, homemade delicious food in a homely and comfortable setting. They serve anything from sandwiched to five course meals and ensure you will be impressed with mouth-watering food they offer. The extensive food and drinks menu also includes some very good diabetic, gluten-free and vegetarian options. Also available is afternoon tea, with homemade cakes served on fine bone china.

The farm shop sells their own dairy produce along with other locally sourced fresh fruit and vegetables, meats, cheese, juice, jam and chutney. There is a selection of homemade ready-to-eat meals, breads, pasties and pies, with a variety of cakes and puddings. This peaceful venue is an equally popular location for business lunches as well as for workmen's brunches, with wellington boots as acceptable as a suit and tie.

Opening times:

Tue to Sun 9am—4pm
(drinks only after 3pm)

 Address and contact details:

Park Farm, Walmersley,
Lancashire BL9 5NP
Telephone: 01706 823 584
www.parkfarmshopramsbottom.co.uk

Directions:

Situated on the A56 from Edenfield to Bury, Park Farm is through Shuttleworth on the left hand side.

"Just had lunch at Park Farm, wonderful as usual would have had a cocktail if not driving!"

The East Lancashire railway operated from 1844–1959 and connected town and cities including Liverpool, Manchester and Blackburn. Now run as a heritage line it host many steam and diesel events and various themed days and excursions.

Photography credit: Paul Grogan Photography

Holden Wood Antiques and Tearoom

Haslingden

The tearoom is situated in the conservatory and serves fresh quality food. An all-day breakfast is available from 8.30am, along with a selection of main meals and daily specials, lighter bites and delicious homemade cakes are served from 11.30am until 4pm. They also offer afternoon tea with freshly baked scones, finger sandwiches, and pot of traditional English or speciality teas.

The antiques centre is set within the church building, and has been established for 20 years. Surrounded by beautiful stone work and stained glass windows, creating an idyllic setting for the many antiquities on display inside. There are collectables, jewellery, furniture, and paintings, along with contemporary pieces from selected artists, potters and sculptors.

Opening times:

Tearoom
Mon to Sun 8.30—5pm
(drinks and cake only after 4pm

Antiques centre
10am—5.30pm

Address and contact details:

Grane Road, Haslingden,
Lancashire BB4 4AT
Telephone: 01706 211 630
www.holdenwood.co.uk

Directions:

Situated on the B6232, from Haslingden to Blackburn. You'll find Holden Wood Antiques and Tearoom just outside Haslingden, immediately after the turning for B6214, on the left.

"Beautiful conversion of a church into an antiques store and tearooms. Great friendly service and top notch food in pleasant atmosphere. Would highly recommend this place for somewhere different for breakfast, brunch or lunch, or maybe just a tea or coffee."

Toffalis Fish and Chip Shop

Crawshawbooth

Toffalis is set in the small village of Crawshawbooth near the market town of Rawstenstall, in the heart of the Rossendale valley. It is a popular walker's destination due to the rugged countryside and wonderful scenery. Toffalis is a family run business that has many years' experience in serving the finest quality fish that is sustainably sourced. They have an extensive menu with options to suit all tastes and appetites, including traditional cod and haddock which is always a local favourite, along with Hollands pies, burgers and all the other extras you would expect. There is a specials board which changes regularly, and all food is made fresh daily.

They can also cater for private parties and special occasions.

Opening times:

Restaurant
Mon 4—6.30pm
Tue to Thurs 11.30am—6.30pm
Fri 11.30am—7pm
Sat 11.30am—6pm
Sun Closed

Address and contact details:

554 Burnley Road, Crawshawbooth,
Rossendale BB4 8NE
Telephone: 01706 212 842
www.toffalisfishbar.co.uk

Directions:

Toffalis is along the A682 from Rawtenstall towards Burnley, about 1½ miles out of Rawtenstall on the left hand side.

∞
THE HALO

The Halo is an 18 metre diameter
sculpture by John Kennedy.
From its position on Top o' Slate,
an old quarry and former landfill
site situated in the hills above
Haslingden in the Rossendale
Valley, it is visible for miles around.

Photography credit: Mike Black Photographer

The Bridge Fish and Chip Shop

Norden (near Rochdale)

The Bridge Fish and Chip shop is one of the finest fish and chip shop in the area. The fish is wonderfully fresh and fried to perfection, the batter is light and crisp, and the fish is succulent and moist inside, each flake just melts in your mouth. This combined with golden chunky chips make the perfect afternoon treat or dinnertime meal.

In the restaurant they have a selection of freshly prepared meals, including homemade steak and ale pie, rag pudding, salmon and homemade chicken curry. A daily specials board which changes regularly, and an OAP special. All may be accompanied by hot and cold beverages including bottled beers and cider. For pudding there is a generous selection of flavoured ice creams, and traditionally tempting cakes to choose from.

 Opening times:

Café
Mon to Sat 11am—8pm
Sun 11am—7pm

Takeaway
Mon to Sat 11am—9pm
Sun 11am—8pm

Address and contact details:

731 Edenfield Road,
Norden, Rochdale OL11 5TT
Telephone: 01706 837 585
www.thebridgechippy.co.uk

Directions:

Situated on the A608 from Rochdale to Edenfield, on the left hand side in Norden.

The Co-operative Deli

Todmorden

The café bar restaurant is easily accessible from the canal, and as such welcomes walker, cyclists, children, and dogs alike. Built in the 1860's, this wonderful building still retains many of its original architectural features, with the café specialising in local seasonal vegetarian and vegan fayre.

Breakfast (served until 11.45am) includes homemade granola, pancakes, potato hash and Shakshuka, a Middle Eastern dish of spiced peppers and tomatoes with a poached egg.

Lunch is a selection of fresh deli salads, and flavoursome seasonal vegetable dishes, all served with locally made bread. The burgers are a real vegetarian feast, along with platters, mezze boards and a selection of daily specials. There are a selection of fabulous homemade cakes and pastries and these can be enjoyed with one of a choice of very good coffees, speciality teas and local beers.

Opening times:

Mon to Sat 9am—5pm
Sun 10am—5pm

Address and contact details:

29 Rochdale Road,
Todmorden OL14 7LA
Telephone: 01706 433 606
www.theoldcoop.com

Directions:

The Co-Op Deli is situated about 5½ miles on the right hand side of the A6033 from Littleborough to Todmorden.

∞

DOVESTONE RESERVOIR

Dovestone Reservoir lies in the convergence of two valleys on the Saddleworth moor. It is on the edge of the Peak District offering walkers many picturesque routes around the area.

Photography credit: David Schofield

Rebecca's Café

Littleborough

Rebecca's is a small and friendly coffee shop situated in Littleborough, near to Hollingworth Lake. They have a lovely cosy corner with sofas to relax on. They serve a light all day breakfast menu offering bacon balm, egg on toast, porridge and other light breakfast fayre. The lunch menu has a selection of baked potatoes, paninis, and sandwiches, along with a variety of daily specials (gluten free options are available).

They have a generous and tempting cake range which changes on a regular basis: red velvet, Victoria sponge, brownies, pies and biscuits, all are homemade and many are gluten free. They also offer afternoon tea which consist of a variety of cakes, accompanied by a pot of tea of filter coffee. There is also an extensive beverage menu.

Opening times:

Mon to Sat 9am—5pm

Address and contact details:

5 Hare Hill Road,
Littleborough OL15 9AB
Telephone: 07957 345 988
www.rebeccascoffeeshop.co.uk

Directions:

Follow the A680 from Edenfield towards Rochdale, continue onto A58 Halifax Road, follow this road for around 2 miles, turn on to Hare Hill Road and Rebecca's is on the left hand side.

Mr Thomas's Fish and Chip Shop

Littleborough

Nestled in the foothills of the south pennies, the little village of Littleborough has many special architectural qualities, and is home to Hollingworth Lake, where sailing windsurfing and rowing take place. Mr Thomas's is situated directly opposite Hollingworth Lake, making it an ideal spot to dine in either before or after taking in the sights.

They have a good selection of fresh fish including cod, haddock and plaice which is lightly battered, crisp and golden, with perfectly cooked chips. They also serve a range of burgers, nuggets and pies. In the café daily specials are available such as homemade fish cakes, lasagne, and many more.

They have a good selection of traditional English puddings including various crumbles, syrup sponge, sticky toffee pudding all served with custard or cream, along with a generous selection of ice creams.

Opening times:

Mon to Sun 11am—8pm

Address and contact details:

21 Little Bank, Littleborough
OL15 0DQ
Telephone: 01706 373 731

Directions:

Follow the A6033 from Todmorden to Littleborough. Pick up the B6225 Mr Thomas's is directly opposite Hollingworth Lake.

∞

SADDLEWORTH VILLAGE

The Yanks weekend is an annual World War II event hosted in Saddleworth. It celebrates the 1979 film Yanks, that Oldham Saddleworth and the surrounding areas were used in the making of.

Photography credit: David Schofield

Betty's Fish and Chip Shop

Uppermill

Betty's is opposite a lovely stretch of the Leeds Liverpool canal, which opened in 1811, its main purpose was the transport of goods from collieries and textile manufacture. Today it is used for pleasure cruising and the Saddleworth canal boat ride pass through Uppermill enroute.

Whether taking a stroll along the canal or a ride on the canal boats, Betty's is the ideal stop for perfect fish and chips. It's a traditional fish and chip shop selling quality fish and chips, to eat in or take away. They have wonderfully fresh lightly battered fish along with plate pies, rag pudding and all the sundries you would expect. If you're feeling really hungry there's the 'big un' which is a 12oz fish. Any of this can be enjoyed with a hot or cold beverage of your choice, including wine and beer.

Opening times:

Mon to Wed 11.30am—2pm, and 4—8pm
Thurs to Sat 11.30am—8pm
Sun 11.30am—4pm

Address and contact details:

36 High Street, Uppermill,
Oldham OL3 6HR
Telephone: 01457 877 100

Directions:

Take the A669 form Oldham towards Huddersfield, continue onto A670 follow this for about a mile, Betty's will be on the left.

The Limekiln Café

Uppermill

One of the most alluring feature of the Limekiln has to be the heated veranda overlooking the Leeds Liverpool canal. On a nice day you can sit and watch canal boats passing through the lock under the viaduct, and if it's a little chill there are blankets to snuggle into. The breakfast fayre can be light and fresh with organic granola or smoothie, through to a full English (and vegetarian full English) there's sure to be something for everyone. The lunch menu has a tempting selection of hot and cold sandwiches, platters for sharing, and mouth-watering daily specials.

Afternoon tea is also available, dainty sandwiches, homemade scones and mini cakes served with award winning loose leaf tea, coffee or prosecco. They also host monthly themed Friday and Saturday night supper clubs, with a different foodie theme for each month.

 Opening times:

Mon to Sun 9am—7pm
Breakfast until 11.30 weekdays,
all day Sat and Sun

Address and contact details:

Brownhill Visitor Centre,
Wool Road, Dobcross,
Saddleworth OL3 5PB
Telephone: 01457 871 051
www.thelimekilncafe.com

Directions:

Take the A669 form Oldham towards Huddersfield, continue onto A670 follow this for about 1½ miles, the Limekiln Café will be on the left hand side.

"Beautiful Café, wonderful food with extensive menu and friendly staff. Lovely to be able to sit outside having something to eat and watching the geese and world go by on the canal. An absolute gem."

∞
MEDIA CITY, SALFORD QUAYS

A favourite tourist hotspot is Media City at Salford Quays. Connected to Manchester via the Metrolink tram system, it is home to ITV, the BBC, the Lowry Arts Centre and Theatre, the Imperial War Museum North and the Lowry Outlet Village.

Photography credit: Paul Grogan Photography

Here are a few recipes that have stood the test of time through many generations of home cooking. Some of these still use the same ingredients today, while others have had unique and subtle changes along the way. These recipes are firm family favourites, which are enjoyed by all on many occasions. We hope you enjoy making them and get as much pleasure from eating and sharing them as we do.

Victoria Greenwood

Beef Casserole

Serves four

Beef casserole is thought to have been invented in Berlin in and consisted of pressed rice, vegetables and meats. Its transition to the modern day form of being cooked in earthenware pots became popular in the early 1900s and was commonly cooked among the working classes throughout England.

Method:

Set the oven to 180°C

Top and tail the carrots, peel and dice the parsnip and potatoes, and roughly chop the celery and leaks. Season the flour well with salt and pepper then toss the beef in it.

Add a drizzle of oil and the butter to the pan, add the sage and beef and fry until the beef starts to take colour. Then add the rest of the veg, herbs red wine beef stock and tomato pure.

Bring to the boil on the hob then cover with a lid and place in the oven for about 3 hours, or until the meat is really tender.

Remove from the oven and serve with fresh crusty bread.

Ingredients:

500g diced stewing beef
500g potatoes
300g Chantenay carrots
2 parsnips
2 celery sticks
2 large leak
2 sprigs of thyme
6 sage leaves
1 bay leaf
200ml red wine
1 pint of beef stock
2 tbsp. tomato puree
4 tbsp. plain flour
Knob of butter

Lancashire Hotpot

This dish has been cooked in Lancashire since before industrialisation, when families would work from home and the dish would cook slowly throughout the day on a low fire. It was traditionally made using mutton which benefited from the slow cooking allowing the meat to become tender.

Method:

Set the oven to 180°C

Dice the lamb leg in to 3cm cubed pieces. Heat the oil in a pan, and fry the lamb until browned on all sides, add the onion and carrot and fry until the onion are slightly soft. Season with salt and pepper. Stir in the flour then add the stock, rosemary and thyme then bring to the boil, and once it begins to thicken, simmer gently.

Peel and slice the potatoes (½cm thick) transfer the mixture from the pan to a casserole dish. Layer the potatoes on top of the mixture and brush with melted butter.

Place a lid on the casserole dish and place in the oven for 2 hours, remove the lid for the last half hour to allow the potatoes to brown.

Check that the lamb is tender by prodding it with a knife if so remove from the oven. Serve with seasonal greens.

Ingredients:

500g lamb leg
500g potatoes
4 large carrots
2 large onions
500ml lamb stock
1 stalk fresh thyme
1 stalk fresh rosemary
3 tbsp. plain flour
Salt and pepper
A couple of knobs of butter
2 tbsp. olive oil

Shepherds Pie

This dish was traditionally made as way to use up left over roast meats of any type, the mash potato was originally used as a base as well as a crust. Today there are many variations of the dish, some include fruit in the filling, while others top it with cheese or breadcrumbs.

Method:

Peel and chop the carrots, dice the onion, and place in a large pan with the mince. Add enough water to cover the mixture and bring to the boil. While this is coming to the boil, peel and chop the potatoes and place them in cold, lightly salted water and boil until softened.

Once the mince mixture comes to the boil, reduce the heat and skim the fat and scum off, then return to simmer. Mix the stock cube with a little boiling water to dissolve it, then add it to the mixture along with the frozen peas, herbs and tomato puree, and simmer for 20 minutes. Season to taste.

When the potatoes have softened, drain them then return to the pan. Add the butter and milk then mash until smooth and creamy. Place the mince mixture in a backing dish and top with the mash potato, place in the oven and bake until golden on top.

Ingredients:

1 white onion
3 carrots
2 sprigs of fresh rosemary
2 sprigs thyme
500g lamb mince
Salt and pepper to season
1 lamb stock cube
1 tbsp. tomato puree
1 cup frozen peas
1.5kg potatoes
100ml milk
Large knob of butter

Fruit Filled Meringue Nest

Makes 10 to 12 portions

Meringue is said to have originated in the Swiss village of Meiringen in the 17th century, but they date back to 1604 in English history with 'White Biskit Bread' being made by Lady Elinor Poole Fettiplace of Gloucestershire. They are still made by the original method and recipe.

Method:

Set the oven to 150°C

In a very clean bowl or stand mixer whisk the egg whites until they form firm peaks. Whilst still mixing gradually add the caster sugar then mix on full power for 5 minutes, or until the mixture is smooth and glossy. Place grease proof paper on a backing tray using a little of the meringue dotted on the tray to stick the paper down.

Fill a piping bag with the meringue and pipe the nest shapes on to the tray starting with the centre of the base working out and up in circular motions. Place the meringues in the oven for 30 minutes or until golden. Once done remove and allow to cool. For the filling whisk the cream and icing sugar together in a bowl until thickened. Once the meringues have cooled spoon a little of the cream into the base of the nests, then decorate with the berries and top with fresh mint leaves, and a drizzle of raspberry coulis.

Ingredients:

Meringue
4 egg whites
200g caster sugar

Filling
250 ml double cream
50g icing sugar
300g fresh mixed berries
Fresh mint
Raspberry coulis (optional)

Apple and plum pie

The earliest recorded recipe for apple pie in England, dates back to 1381. However the ingredients used were somewhat different from modern methods. Figs, raisins, and pears were added as well as apples, to sweeten the pie, as sugar was very expensive and not readily available.

Method:

Preheat oven at 200°C Add the flour, butter and lard to a blender and pulse until it forms a breadcrumb consistency then add the icing sugar. Next add the egg and mix until it combines, if it is still a little dry add a few drops of water to bring it together. Remove from the blender and divide in two equal halves, wrap half in clingfilm and place in the fridge. Roll out the other half on a lightly floured surface that is wide enough to line your pie dish, then grease and line it with the pastry. Make sure you leave some overhanging. Place it in the fridge to chill while you make the filling.

Peel and core the apples and roughly slice them, placing them in a bowl with a little sprinkle of sugar as you go to prevent them browning. Skin, de-stone and chop the plums, then add them to the bowl with a little more sugar to taste and mix, then add the corn flour and coat the fruit. Remove the lined dish from the fridge and add the filling, next roll out the remainder of the pastry large enough to cover the pie, cut any excess off and pinch the two pastry edges together. Brush with a little milk, decorate with shape cut from the left over pastry, sprinkle with a little sugar and bake at 200°C of 15 minutes than reduce to 180°C for a further 25–30 minutes until the pie is golden and the filling is soft.

Remove from the oven and serve with cream or custard.

Ingredients:

350g plain flour
90g hard butter cubed
85g hard lard cubed
50g icing sugar
1 egg beaten
2 tbsp. water
900g eating apples
400g plums
1 tbsp. cornflour
Granulated sugar to taste

Victoria Sponge

According to certain food historians, cake in Victorian times would have been a heavy cake filled with fruit and nuts. But this is thought to be dangerous for small children to eat. Therefore Victoria sponge cake it thought to have originated as a nursery cake for toddler to enjoy, and later came into popular demand by adults.

Method:

Set the oven to 180°C

Line the two cake tins with grease proof paper.

Place all the cake ingredients in a mixing bowl and combine using an electric whisk until smooth and creamy.

Separate the mixture equally between the two cake tins. Place in the oven and cook for 20–25 minutes, until golden and when pricked with a skewer the skewer comes out clean. Remove from the oven and leave to cool on a cooling rack.

Once completely cooled, place the butter in a mixing bowl and beat until creamy. Next add half the caster sugar and combine until smooth, then add the rest and mix again. If the mixture is to stiff add 2–3 table spoons of milk.

Take the bottom sponge and spread the jam onto it. Next fill a piping bag with the buttercream and pipe it on top of the jam, or it can be spread on the top sponge if preferred.

Finally place the top sponge on top of the bottom sponge and dust with icing sugar to finish.

Ingredients:

Cake
250g self raising flour
250g margarine
250g caster sugar
4 eggs
1 tsp. baking powder
1 vanilla pod seeds only or 1 tsp.
Vanilla extract

Filling
250g soft butter
250g icing sugar
2-3 tbsp. milk
300g good quality strawberry jam

YOUR VOUCHERS

Dining in all of these cafés will be an enjoyable experience on any occasion. The use of fresh local produce, seasonal menus, and amazing desserts, ensures each visit is never quite the same.

Please use these vouches at any of the cafés featured in the book, and enjoy dining for a little less.

Café Culture

∞
THE LUNE ESTUARY

The Lune Estuary dominates the area and the coastal trail includes an old port, a lighthouse and monastic remains overlooking the atmospheric Lancashire Coast and magnificent Morecambe Bay.

Photography credit: Paul Grogan Photography

MAP INDEX

1. Arnside Chip Shop and the Big Chip Café
    1 The Promenade, Arnside, Carnforth LA5 0HF
    Telephone: 01524 761 874

2. RSPB Leighton Moss Café
    Myers Farm, Storrs Lane, Silverdale, LA5 0SW
    Telephone: 01524 701 601

3. Greenlands Farm Village
    Tewitfield, Carnforth, Lancashire LA6 1JH
    Telephone: 01524 784 184

4. Countrystyle Meats Farm Shop
    Lancaster Leisure Park, Wyresdale Road, Lancaster LA1 3LA
    Telephone: 01524 841 111

5. Bridge House Farm
    Bridge House, Lancaster, LA2 8QP
    Telephone: 01524 222 496

6. Pilling Pottery
    School Lane, Pilling, Garstang, Lancashire PR3 6HB
    Telephone: 01253 799 928

7. The Fish House
    172-180 Dock Street, Fleetwood FY7 6NY
    Telephone: 01253 779229

    The Fish Hut,
    294A Poulton Road, Fleetwood FY7 6TF

8. St. Annes Fish Restaurant
    41 St Andrew's Road South, Lytham St. Annes FY8 1PZ
    Telephone: 01253 723 311

9. The Courtyard Caffé
    17 High Street, Great Eccleston, Preston, PR3 0ZB
    Telephone: 01995 672 011

10. Light Ash Farm
    St Michael's Road, Bilsborrow, Preston PR3 0RT
    Telephone: 01995 640 068

11. Garstang Fish and Chip Shop
    Stoops Hall Wind, Garstang, Preston PR3 1EA
    Telephone: 01995 600 205

12. Cobble Hey Farm and Gardens
    Forest of Bowland AONB, Hobbs Lane, Claughton-on-Brock, Garstang, Preston PR3 0QN
    Telephone: 01995 602 643